T0368480

YOGA
FOR CHILDREN
– AND THEIR FAMILIES

Tanja Krogh Pedersen

Balboa Press books may be ordered through booksellers or by contacting:

Balboa Press
A Division of Hay House
1663 Liberty Drive
Bloomington, IN 47403
www.balboapress.com
844-682-1282

Illustrated by
Tanja Krogh Pedersen - animal illustrations and
Anastasia Marianna Hansen - character illustrations

ISBN: 979-8-7652-3821-9 (sc)
ISBN: 979-8-7652-3601-7 (e)

Library of Congress Control Number: 2023901232

Print information available on the last page.

Balboa Press rev. date: 05/09/2023

Contents

Yoga for children

Yoga for children has been adapted to their growing bodies.

They will learn about themselves and their bodies and develop mental and physical strength and flexibility. Through this, they will gain self-confidence in a fun and playful way.

This book contains a variety of yoga exercises and mindfulness exercises presented in a creative and playful way - which is a great way to learn.

There are rhymes and a couple of songs to make it special for the children.

Children learn faster with a combination of rhyme, rhythm and movement.

And they will also be able to hold a pose longer when they have a rhyme to focus on.

The rhymes stimulate their language, and the story and mindfulness exercises will increase their creativity and ability to visualize pictures.

Some of the benefits of yoga for children:

- Body awareness and joy for the body, movement and learning
- Support to strengthen the body, balance and enhance their motoric development
- Improve flexibility of the body and mind
- Endurance
- Patience
- Honesty towards themselves and others
- Inner peace
- Increase their ability to feel themselves – and to realize when they need to take a break
- Improve creativity
- Empathy towards relations, friends, nature and animals
- Improve their ability to adapt emotions
- Enhance their focus and concentration
- Relax their body and mind
- Better sleep

How to use this book

Learning yoga should be a fun, encouraging and playful experience.

When you teach children from age 3-5 years, you should not correct them.

Allow the children to have fun and play and discover their bodies, balance, minds and mood. When this is done in a playful way, it encourages their willingness to learn and their ability to adapt emotions.

Children aged 3-5 enjoy repetition – so they can easily perform the same sequence up to about 5 times until you move on to new positions.

Children aged 6–9 may receive small corrections.

Remember always to be kind and supportive.

The best way to introduce yoga for your children is to read the book for them as a story.

Then you can introduce one exercise at a time – or make smaller sequences introducing a couple of positions at a time.

Here are smaller sequences that take about 5-15 min.

One part of the book is written as a whole class in story form, which takes around 45 min.

This class starts with easier exercises and then becomes more challenging, and it is made up of different activity levels.

You can teach the book one on one or to a group of up to 16 children at a time.

You can practice the different exercises according to what feels good for you that day.

Remember to do the exercises on both sides of the body.

During yoga you can talk to the children about the different animals, trees and permaculture. There are some facts about all this at the end of the book. You can introduce one fact every time you do the exercise.

Healthy habits

Benefits: makes you feel good and safe

I place a hand on my stomach and a hand on my heart
Today I want a good start

I will eat a healthy breakfast today
So I have energy to play

It's also food for my brain
So I can learn and obtain

I like to eat healthy food
It keeps me in a good mood

The yoga button

Benefits: relaxation and attention

This exercise is used to prepare the student for the yoga class.

It creates focus, attention, concentration and raises the energy level during yoga.

On top of my head
There is a point I can press
I massage it and press
Then I take a deep breath

When my yoga button is released
I am relaxed and at ease

It makes my spine grow long
And my heart opens up strong

With an open heart I am ready to start

You can always press this button when you need a little energy boost and to remind yourself about your yoga practice.

Sun salutation (3-5 years)

Instruction: Do like me

a Thank you,

b I feel the strength

f - And I roll up and stand tall as a tree

e- I feel your warmth inside me

d -It makes me feel

dear Sun

within me

Benefits: It is a great way to start the day; strech the body after sleeping; move, energize and wake up your body, mind and soul.

b - Waking up is fun

c- When I see your light and feel your warmth

so strong

Sun salutation (6-9 years)

Instructions: On page 7

Begin in the top and follow the illustrations clockwise around the sun.

1 Thank you

12 And I feel the

11 I stand tall as a tree

10 I feel the gentle breeze

9 Wake up with ease

8 Dogs, birds, bees, plants and trees

7 Who is looking for prey?
Raise and sway
Say "sss" (like a snake)

for today

strengh within me

Benefits: It is a great way to start the day; stretch the body after sleeping; move, energize and wake up your body, mind and soul.

2 Thank you, dear sun

3 Waking up is fun

4 When I see your light and feel your warmth

5. It makes me feel so strong

6 Now I'll take a break

1 Stand tall and place your palms against each other in front of your heart.

2 Stretch tall, reach for the sun, your palms towards each other and look up.

3 Bow your head and roll gently and slowly forwards, until your hands touch the floor, or as far as you can get, it should feel comfortable for you. You might want a slight bend in your knees.

4 Bend your knees and bottom out.

5 Make a gentle jump, into the plank, your toes on the floor, your stomach up, don't let it hang.

Bottom in line with your body.

6 Lie down on your stomach, hands on the floor, next to the chest.

7 Place your toes on the floor.

8 Bottom out and push yourself into downward dog with your hands. Stand with the whole hand on the floor.

9 Walk your feet to your hands or make a gentle jump, hands around your ankles and bottom out. Look in front of you.

10 Walk your hands forward, under your shoulders and straighten your legs.

Make a small bend in your knees and let your head hang.

11 Stretch tall, reach for the sun, your palms towards each other and look up.

12 Stand tall and place your palms against each other in front of your heart.

The whole class begins here:

You can also do each exercise on its own, or combine them in shorter sequences.

Body awareness

Rub your hands against each other until they are warm and place them under the soles of your feet, and then repeat and place them around your knee.

Start in the middle before each exercise, go to the top and follow the illustrations clockwise around.

Cover your eyes with your

hands, then remove your hands.

Notice the color in front of your eyes

Repeat and place your hands
around your other knee

Feel the warmth
and your breath

Feel your heartbeat

Introduction to Sthira

Sthira means strength and steadiness in your:

- body

- mind

- breathing (strong and steady flow in the breath).

Talk about examples.

Do you know this feeling?

Do you remember a situation where you used strength or steadiness?

Or maybe both together?

Are you ready to come with me on a yoga journey?

We will begin in nature at the edge of a forest, on a field of grass with flowers.

Message from the Butterfly:

My message to you is a message of joy.
Feel the joy everywhere you move, be joyful.

The Butterfly

Let's sit in The Butterfly

Instructions:

3-5 years: Sit like me

6 and up: Soles against each other, knees bent.

All: Press the yoga button on top of your head so your back grows tall and chest opens.

Benefits: hip opener and grounding, flexibility for the spine, core and lubrication of joints.

Precautions: Do not overbend your knees.

You can move your feet forward to make the bend more gentle.

The butterfly is sitting in the grass next to me
And I mimic the fluttering wings with my knees

Up and down – first slow
Gently faster as it gets ready to go

It's flying over the grass with its wing power
To the sweet nectar in the flowers

The Flower

Instructions:

3-5 years: Do like me

6 years and up:

Take one ankle with the opposite hand and place your leg in your bent arm.

Lift the other leg and place it in the bent arm on the same side.

Play with your balance; you can put your feet together or draw the legs apart from each other; play with your strength and balance.

Benifits: Balance, core power and back strength

The butterfly takes off and passes a dog

Message from the dog :

My message to you is a message of something I appreciate and which makes me feel good.

It's good to have a small task to perform
To experience that you are in charge of something special

The Downward Dog

Instruction:

3-5 years: Do like me

6 years and up:

Legs on the floor, again on all fours, and stretch the legs, move your bottom towards the wall, so you resemble a upside-down V.

Benefits: Strengthen and stretch the legs, back, shoulders and arms, and send blood to the brain.

Precautions: Stand on the whole hand.

The dog is peeing.

Bend and lift one leg off the floor and make the sound "ttsssssss".

Change to the other leg and repeat.

Now the butterfly likes to rest and finds a "forest bed"

Reclined Buttefly

3-5 years: Do like me. Help them to support their legs with pillows or folded blankets.

6 years and up:

Lie on your back and bend your knees and put your soles together; let your knees fall gently towards the floor – you can also support the knees with 2 pillows.

Interlace your fingers behind your head (3-6 years)

Hold on to opposite elbow. Stay here (6-11 years)

Benefits: Stretches the inside of the thighs, psoas, chest, shoulders and back in a gentle way; it also releases anger and distress and relaxes psoas – when it is supported.

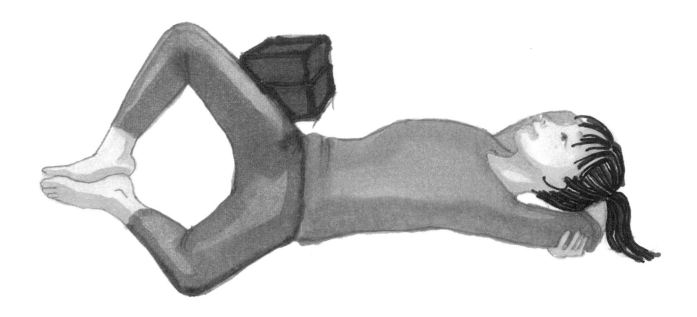

Hold this position for 2-3 minutes.

You can end the yoga program here or continue to the next part of the story.

Now we are ready to go into the forest.

The message from the tree is:

There are things you cannot do alone, in those situations stand together and help each other as friends.

And you have to allow yourself to play.

Let us stand up and run in place.

Run in place or around the room for 2 minutes.

Stop.

I place my hand on my heart and feel it beating fast

I place a hand on my stomach and feel my breath is fast

As I stand still for a while taking a rest

I feel my heartbeat slowing down together with my breath

The Tree

Instructions:

3-5 years: Do like me

6 years and up:

Stand on the ground and press the yoga button on top of your head.

Place one foot on the inside of the opposite leg above or below the knee joint.

Find a point to look at on the floor in front of you.

Then try the different variations.

Benefits: Balance, strength and steadiness

Precautions: Do not place your foot directly on the knee joint – place it above or below.

In the forest there is a tree
and I feel its energy

I stand tall as the tree
I lift and bend one knee

As I stand as the tree
I feel the Sthira inside of me

Change to the other leg.

The tree visualization

Visualization:

Is there anything you can do so you can stand longer or more stable?

Try to imagine that you are the tree and have roots from your feet down into the ground supporting you.

Did this visualization make a difference for you?

How did it make you feel?

When you have played with the different variations or simply been in the tree pose, place your foot on the ground and your hands along your sides.

Roll forward and walk the hands forward so you are in downward dog.

The message from the Lizard:

Remember to dream and
Listen to your own inner voice

The Lizard is for children from 6 years and up; if you are 3-5 years, go to the dove.

Suddenly I hear a sound
It is a Lizard running across the ground

Benefits: Balance, steadiness, strengthen the legs, hip opener

The Lizard

Instructions:

You are in downward dog and from this position step forward with your right leg on the outside of your right hand.

Breathe in this position 3-4 times.
And step back to downward dog.

Step forward with your leg and place your foot on the outside of your left hand.
Breathe 3-4 times.
Then step back into downward dog.

Message from the Dove

My message for you is,

Remember the gentle support.

Help each other.

Choose to have friends around you who believe in you – sot that you are supported and you can do what you set out to do.

From above in the tree,

I see a dove looking down on me

The dove

Benefits: coordination, flexibility
of the hip joint and hip opener

instruction:

3-5 years: Do like me

Then back on all fours and remember to do the same on the other side.

6-9 years:

Come down on all fours.

Place your right knee behind your right wrist.

The leg is sideways on the mat, slide back on your left knee until you feel a stretch in your buttock.

If you are falling a bit sideways, make sure you fall towards the side with the straight leg.

Breathe for a couple of moments in this position and come out into downward dog.

Then back on all fours and remember to do the same on the other side.

Message from the Bumble Bee:

It is powerful to be present and full of life energy
It is powerful to be gentle and to have compassion

The Bumble Bee

Instructions:

3-5 years: Do like me

6 years and up:

Sit cross-legged and press your yoga button on top of your head.

Benefits: Calms an agitated mind, stimulates the vagus nerve, boosts the immune system, relaxes the nervous system, regulates metabolism and many more good effects.

Bumble Bee, Bumble Bee

You are a friend to me

Flying from flower to flower

With your mighty wing power

Sit on your bottom.

Close your eyes and ears.

Breathe in through your nose.

Your lips are gently closed.

And make the sound "M" like the Bumble Bee,

for as long as it feels good.

Continue on and off for about 5 minutes.

Children and adults concentrate on their own rhythms – this is part of the training in this fun exercise.

(to be continued on the next page)

Then sit for a while and feel the sensation. Feel the sound vibrating in your body and cheeks, and feel the warmth and the tingling sensations, maybe even well-being.

How to make a thought bottle:

- A transparent bottle with a good lid
- 4 dl pure neutral glycerin
- 5-6 dl water
- Glitter in different colors
- 5-10 drops of transparent dishwashing liquid

For inspiration:

Green and gold for imagination, creativity, calming.

Blue and green to imitate the sea or a lake.

Blue and silver to imitate the night sky.

Make up your own.

We gather in a circle :

Thought bottle

This is a peaceful exercise, so we are silent.
Shake it and sit silently watching the glitter settling on the bottom.

I am upset and I like to clear my head
My thoughts are twirling – as if I was an angry whirlwind

I watch the glitter in the bottle without a sound
Moving up and down and around

As the glitter settles at the bottom or at the top
The whirlwind has given up

Now I can express
What made me upset

I like to take a break
And therefore I shake

The glitter is dancing and twirling
I look at it with my eyes, and it makes me mesmerized
I can easily breathe and connect to inner peace
I feel myself with ease and my creativity is released

The cotton ball song

Tanja Krogh Pedersen

I place a cottonball in your hand
Now blow it from where you stand

Now here's a straw
Blow through that once more

Lift it from the floor
and hold it with the straw

Blow hard or soft
and watch it take off

You hold it as long as you can
and blow it to a spot you plan

31

Play with cotton ball and a straw

Benefits: Good for practicing breathing.

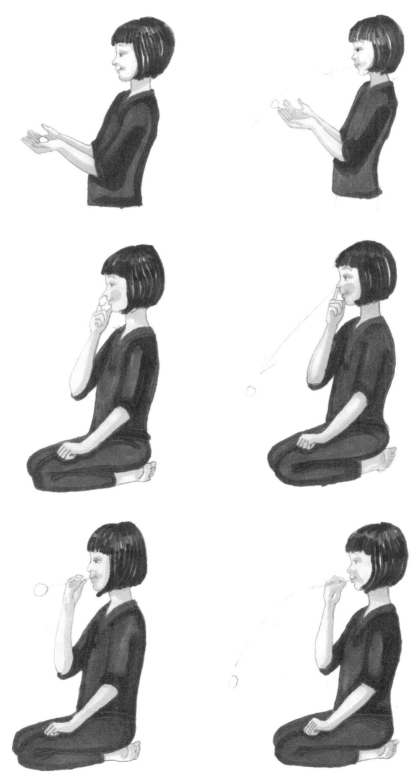

To be continued on the next page

You can blow through your mouth.

You can blow and inhale through your nostrils – one at a time.

You can blow through a straw.

Make a line at one end of the room and blow the cotton ball across the room and across the line – and back.

This is also fun when you are more than one.

There are many ways to play this game – use your imagination.

The Child's pose

Instructions :

3-5 years: Do like me

6 years and up:

Place your bottom on your heels.

And place your forehead on the floor.

You can spread your knees if it is more comfortable.

Benefits: Hip opener, forward bend and calming

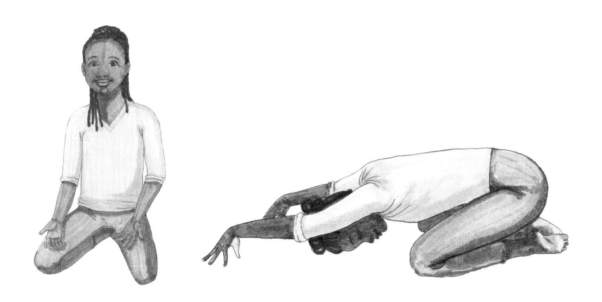

Place your hands above your head with your fingers on the floor – breathe.

Take a deep breath through your nose and down into your belly.

And let your back expand and become wide – and take your space.

Take your place in this world.

Stay in this position for 2 minutes.

The message from the elephant is:

You can become as strong as me.

Find the way through your heart.

Through the love of life find your willpower, and this will be your strength.

The elephant massage song

Tanja Krogh Pedersen

I'll splash you with water
It's easy 'cause you are shorter

Then I move to your side
Don't try to hide

I'll massage your back with soap
This gives so much hope

I'll splash you clean with water
It's easy 'cause you are shorter

I'll dry your back
So you can relax

Cool down massage sequence

Now we are partnered up two and two. Agree on who will receive a massage first and who will give first.

After the first round you will change places, so the one who gave will receive and the one who received will give.

The one who will receive a massage lies down on the stomach.

Sitting by the head and making long strokes from the shoulders to the lower back.

(Effleurage)

singing (optional)

"I'll splash you with some water

This is easy 'cause you're shorter"

Move to the side

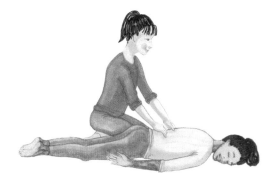

kneed the side of the body (from the hip to the ribcage)

"Then move to the side

Don't try to hide"

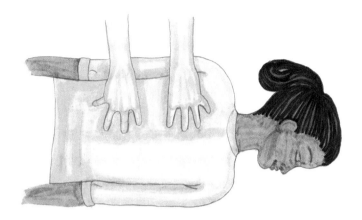

Use your fingertips to massage the whole back and around the shoulders.

"I'll massage your back with soap

This gives so much hope"

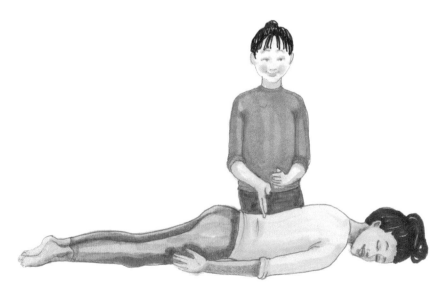

Tapping with the sides of your hands, chop gently up on top of their shoulders and back down (only on the muscles; not on the bones).

"Ill splash you clean with water it's easy 'cause you are shorter"

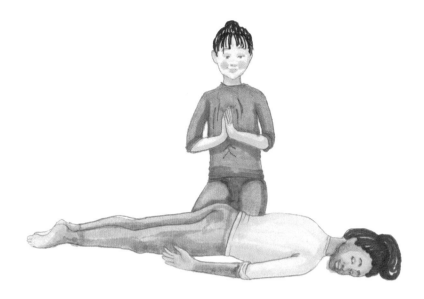

Take a deep breath down into your stomach, and rub your palms against each other until they are warm.

"I'll dry your back"

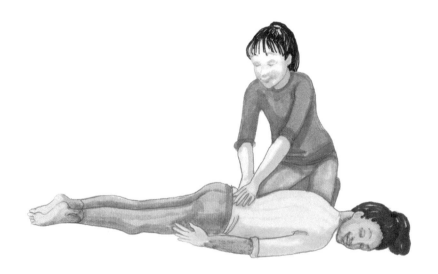

Place them on their lower back.

Then with flat hands crisscross over their back, up and down their back once.

"So you can relax"

Visualization/mindfulness exercise

Benefit: deep relaxation

Now we are going on a visualization exercise.

Lie down comfortably on your back with a blanket over you, and place something over your eyes.

You are walking on the side of a road – there are cars and bikes passing by.

On your righthand side is a small forest, and the sun is shining down from the other side of the forest.

You see a small path of soil and leaves, and you walk on the path into the forest.

You come to a clearing where there is a big old tree, and you walk around it and notice it has an opening. It is possible to walk into the hollow tree through the opening.

Inside, you find a room made for you. It is a quiet room, which you can decorate as you like, and you can talk to the tree.

It is a place where you can go to be on your own.

You can talk to the tree about anything you like; whatever you have on your mind.

You can see the sunlight shining down on you through the top of the tree, and you can feel it's warm and healing light on your body.

Visualization/mindfulness continued

3-5 years:

The sun warms your right foot and lower leg, your right knee and thigh – every single muscle.

The sun warms your left foot and lower leg, your left knee and thigh – every single muscle.

It warms your buttocks and your entire back.

It warms your right arm out to the hand and fingers and your left arm out to the hand and fingers.

It warms your neck, the back of your head and your face and chest, lungs and your stomach – the whole back side and front side of your body.

6 years and up:

4 minutes of silence

For everyone:

Know this is a place you can always return to.

After a while you can walk out of the tree.

Sit up and be present in this room again.

Gratitude

Ending ritual: Form a circle and place your hands in front of your heart and say 1-3 things you are grateful for.

End of class

Message from the Lion:

Find courage and strength in your heart.
Courage to speak your truth.
And the strength to do the things in life you set out to do.

Lion Pose

3-5 years: Do like me

6 years and up:

Benefits: stretches the neck and face, eye motoric function and releases frustrations.

I sit on my knees and they are open. My hands in-between my knees on the floor, with the fingers pointing towards me. Wrists pointing forwards.

I look towards my nose, stick out my tongue and roar like a lion.

The sound comes all the way from the stomach and out through my mouth.

When I am upset

Thoughts are flying through my head

My stomach is tense

And I find it hard to talk to my friends

Even if it seems like a silly pose
Inside of me the Lion rose

My stomach feels warm and at ease
And I feel more at peace

I talk to someone that I can trust
About what I wanted to adjust

Now I can easily express
What made me feel so upset

Here are some facts about animals and trees in this book that you can talk about – just take one fact at a time – not all at once – it is meant as an inspiration and great to talk about while practicing yoga.

Butterflies:

- Live in four stages: Egg, caterpillar, cocoon, and as an insect.
- Some butterflies only live for 3-5 days other butterflies lives longer.
- With a short lifespan, the life of the butterfly is all about propagation.
- Most butterflies live 2-4 weeks.
- The common brimstone lives 9-10 months.
- The butterflies that can survive winter live the longest.

Dogs:

- Are a descendant of the big wolf.
- Are mainly domesticated.
- Their personality and abilities vary according to their breed and training.

Doves:

Are very related to woods, trees and nature.

- They come in many sizes from small as a house sparrow to big as a Turkey.
- They are multi-coloured, all green, and grey and many other colour variations.
- Since the time of the ancient Egyptian, they have been used as letter carriers, because they can always find their way home within a distance of 1100 km.
- They are found all over the world – except in Antarctica and arctic and desert areas, where there is no food for them.

Elephants:

- Live in herds.
- Sense vibrations through their big feet, which give them lots of information.
- They wash and comfort each other.
- They have a good memory and remember everyone they have met – even just once.

Bumble Bees:

- It can carry 60 % of its own weight.
- It only lives for one summer.

- It is only the queen who survives the winter.
- They cannot tolerate pesticides and toxins.
- They mainly like wild flowers.
- We cherish them because they are pollinators.
- What can we do to protect them?

Lions:

- They are the most sociable of all the big cat species.
- They live in prides in the wild, with around 10-15 in each pride.
- It is primarily the lioness who hunts while the lion guards their territory- protecting the pride.
- The lioness enjoys being together with her cubs.
- They can hear their cub calling from a very long distance.
- A lion lives for about 14 years in the wild.

Lizards (Fiji Lizard):

- They are most active in the sun.
- They are ectotherms, which means their bodies assume the temperature of their environment.
- Some are great swimmers, and others live on land.
- Some are vegetarians, and others eat meat.

Trees:

- They form friendships with other trees.
- They live with their tree children.
- Trees have memories.
- They are most productive when they live together in a natural environment- without much human interference.
- They are home to many animals.
- A tree can take care of another tree when it is sick by sharing its nutrients.

Introduction to Permaculture

I would like to tell you about Permaculture. Some of you already know about it, while others will hear about it for the first time.

I hope you will be inspired and start some projects with your family and friends.

Watching plants grow gives a lot of perspective in your life and is a great experience. It takes longer than going to the supermarket to buy vegetables and it requires a lot of water. It is great to know.

The concept of permaculture was introduced by two Australians, Bill Mollison and David Holmgreen in the 1970s.

You can use simple tools to make a sustainable organic system that works with nature – not against it.

With these tools, we create circular systems that enhance nature's resources, such as water, air and soil.

We also enhance ourselves by nurturing our physical, psychological, and spiritual needs, and by working outside with the soil in a sustainable, non-toxic environment.

We make gardens and farms without pesticides and toxins.

When we cooperate, we all benefit from each other's knowledge and experience and create safe and comfortable conditions for ourselves and our surroundings and the next generations.

By distributing the earth's resources equally, we will ensure that everyone benefits from the earth without harming nature, animals, plants, and people.

This is an ethically sound way to live and to nurture the planet we live on and like to live off.

There are permaculture gardens, farms and also forest gardens.

Here is how to make your own forest garden:

In the forest garden, you mimic a native forest, with its many layers that all work together to produce the highest possible yield.

A forest garden is easy to plant anywhere in the backyard or courtyard, and it provides berries, nuts, herbs, and other good greens. It also provides nutrition to bees and butterflies, and it attract othet pollinators.

Your forest garden can look like this:

Perennial fruit and nut trees

Berry bushes

Flowers that attract pollinators or are edible

Herbs

You plant them close together – and in several layers – so they will produce the highest yield and to imitate a natural and steady forest.

When you plant for the bees, humming bees and butterflies, keep in mind that they do not tolerate chemical toxins and pesticides.

Flowers for butterflies:

Scabiosa columbaria – Butterfly Blue, pincushion flower

Knautia arvensis – Blue hat, field scabious

Cirsium palustre – marsh thistle

Bees prefer wildflowers such as cloves, violets, nettles, daisies, etc.

See an example of a forest garden on page 27.

Special thanks to

All my friends and family who supported me during my writing.

Balboa Press, especially Danny Barnes who believed in me.

The animals who are my teachers and who contributed to this book.

Also to all the people with a passion for the environment and animals I talked to when I was collecting material for this book.

Thank you to all my teachers in yoga for children and to all my teachers in animal communication.

Sources:

Danish Ornithological Society
Danish Carrier Pidgeon Association
Danish Society for Nature Conservation
Peter Wohlleben: The Hidden Life of Trees
Worldanimalprotection.dk

Printed in the United States
by Baker & Taylor Publisher Services